Cats of the Wild

ALICE TWINE

PowerKiDS
press™

New York

For Sean and Katie Keating

Published in 2008 by The Rosen Publishing Group, Inc.
29 East 21st Street, New York, NY 10010

First Edition

Editor: Amelie von Zumbusch
Book Design: Julio Gil
Photo Researcher: Nicole Pristash

Photo Credits: Cover, p. 1 © Andy Rouse/Getty Images; pp. 5, 9, 11, 17, 19, 21, 23, 24 (bottom left, top right, bottom right) © www.shutterstock.com; p. 7 © istockphoto.com/Tom Marvin; pp. 13, 24 (top left) © Getty Images; p. 15 © Eric Meola/Getty Images.

Library of Congress Cataloging-in-Publication Data

Twine, Alice.
  Cats of the wild / Alice Twine. — 1st ed.
      p. cm. — (Baby animals)
  Includes index.
  ISBN-13: 978-1-4042-3772-8 (library binding)
  ISBN-10: 1-4042-3772-0 (library binding)
  1. Felidae—Infancy—Juvenile literature. I. Title.
  QL737.C23T85 2008
  599.75—dc22
                                                2006037221

Manufactured in the United States of America

Contents

The babies of big, wild cats, like lions, are most often called cubs.

Cat cubs open their eyes about a week after they are born. Cubs, like this tiger, often have blue eyes.

Mothers take care of their cubs. Cubs drink their mother's milk.

Tiger cubs have **stripes**, just as adult tigers do. The stripes on each tiger are a little bit different.

These cubs are cheetahs. Cheetah cubs have a **mantle** of long, gray fur covering their backs.

Lion cubs live in big family groups, called prides. The members of a pride work together to care for the cubs.

Cat cubs play a lot. They **wrestle** with their brothers and sisters.

Cubs, like this cheetah, chase and **stalk** each other. This is how cubs learn to hunt.

19

All that chasing and playing makes cat cubs sleepy. Cubs take lots of naps.

Wild cats grow up more quickly than people do. Cubs leave their mothers when they are one and a half to four years old.

Words to Know

mantle

stalk

stripes

wrestle

Web Sites

Due to the changing nature of Internet links, PowerKids Press has developed an online list of Web sites related to the subject of this book. This site is updated regularly. Please use this link to access the list: www.powerkidslinks.com/baby/wcats/

24